Geckos

By W. P. Mara

CAPSTONE PRESS

MANKATO, MINNESOTA

C A P S T O N E   P R E S S

818 North Willow Street • Mankato, Minnesota 56001

Printed in the United States of America.

Library of Congress Cataloging-in-Publication Data
Mara, W. P.
    Geckos/by William P. Mara
    p. cm.
    Includes bibliographical references and index.
    Summary: Describes the physical characteristics, habitat, and behavior of the gecko lizard.
    ISBN 1-56065-427-9
    1. Geckos--Juvenile literature. [1. Geckos.] I. Title.
QL666.L245M37 1996
597.95--dc20

                      96-20749
                      CIP
                      AC

Photo credits
Marian Bacon, cover, 4. R.D. Bartlett, 6-13, 22, 26, 30, 32.
W.P. Mara, 17, 19, 25, 34, 36, 43, 47.
James P. Rowan, 14, 20, 28, 39.

Table of Contents

Fast Facts About Geckos 4

Chapter 1   Beautiful Lizards 7

Chapter 2   Where Geckos Live 11

Chapter 3   The Gecko Body 15

Chapter 4   Daily Life 23

Chapter 5   Reproduction 27

Chapter 6   Conservation............................... 33

Range Map.. 12

Photo Diagram 28

Zoos to Visit 38

Glossary 40

To Learn More 42

Useful Addresses 44

Internet Sites 46

Index 48

Words in **boldface** type in the text are defined
in the Glossary in the back of this book.

Fast Facts About Geckos

Scientific Name: Geckos are lizards. Most belong to a family called Gekkonidae.

Physical Features: Geckos vary in length from about two inches (five centimeters) to 15 inches (38 centimeters). Most have heads that seem too large for their bodies. Their skin is very delicate. It is sometimes very colorful. They have toe pads with rows of plates called lamellae. These are covered with microscopic hooks.

Reproduction: Geckos mate in the spring and fall in the northern part of their **range**. They mate any time of year in southern areas. A mother will lay one or two eggs per clutch. The eggs take from two to six months to hatch.

Daily Habits: Most geckos are active during the night and sleep during the day. A few geckos are active during the day. Most geckos live in trees. A few live on the ground.

Range: Geckos live on every continent except Antarctica.

Habitat: Geckos are found in a wide variety of habitats. They live in deserts, rain forests, mountains, and urban areas.

Life Span: Geckos can live from four to 12 years. The oldest gecko on record lived 23 years

Food: Geckos are **carnivores**. Their diet includes beetles, ants, flies, spiders, and crickets. When they are thirsty, they drink drops of water from plant leaves. Some also lap up the juices from broken fruits.

Chapter 1

Beautiful Lizards

Geckos are beautiful lizards. They have been around for a long time. Most scientists believe they first appeared on earth more than 50 million years ago.

Geckos are fairly small and very fast. Most geckos are friendly if you just look at them. But they will probably bite you if you try to pick them up. Geckos are smart hunters and bold fighters. They have survived in a changing world where many other animals have died out.

The word gecko is based on the Malaysian word gekok. The name was given to geckos because some of them made a chirping noise that sounded like the word.

Classification System

Geckos are a part of the **scientific classification system**. The system can be

Geckos are small and fast.

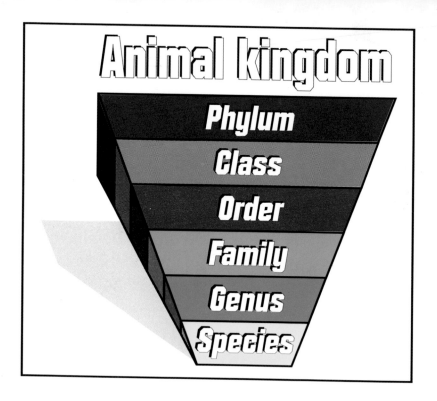

Animal kingdom

Phylum

Class

Order

Family

Genus

Species

thought of as an upside-down pyramid.
Animals that are most closely related are at the
bottom. The largest animal groups are at the
top.

At the very top is a huge group known as a
phylum. Geckos belong to the Chordate
phylum. Just below that is a **class**. Geckos
belong to the Reptile class. Then, there is an
order. Geckos belong to an order with snakes

and other lizards. The name of the order is Squamata (skwa-MAH-tuh).

After that, there is a **family**. Geckos belong to the Gekkonidae (gekk-ON-ih-dee) family. There are 80 smaller groups within the Gekkonidae family. Each of these is called a **genus**. Finally, at the very bottom, is a **species**. There are more than 800 species of geckos.

Common Names

Each gecko has its own Latin name and English name. The Latin name is known as the scientific name. The English name is usually called the common name.

Common names often are based on where a gecko is found. There is the Amazon gecko and the Saint George Island gecko. Other names refer to something about the gecko's appearance. For example, there is the bow-fingered gecko.

Chapter 2

Where Geckos Live

Geckos live in warm areas in many different parts of the world. There are gecko species on every continent but one. They do not live on Antarctica because it is too cold for reptiles there.

Geckos live in the **New World** and the **Old World**. Think of the earth as being divided in half, from top to bottom. The half that contains North America and South America is the New World. The half that contains Europe, Asia, Africa, and Australia is the Old World.

Geckos like to live where it is warm.

Where geckos live

Different Habitats

Geckos live in a variety of **habitats**. They live in rain forests that are moist and humid. They live in deserts that are dry. They live near water and far away from it. Most geckos live in trees and bushes. But they also can be found in open meadows and on mountains.

Some geckos have even learned to live with people. Geckos are often seen scurrying up the sides of buildings and houses in search of insects to eat.

Some geckos live near people.

Chapter 3
The Gecko Body

Geckos are moderate-sized lizards. The smallest gecko is about two inches (five centimeters) long. Large geckos grow to about 15 inches (38 centimeters) long.

The largest gecko in history was the giant gecko of New Zealand. Experts believe it was about two feet (60 centimeters) long.

Most geckos have heads that are fairly large in comparison to the rest of their bodies. They have bulging eyes and a rounded snout. They have a wide mouth with two rows of sharp teeth.

Most geckos have bulging eyes and a rounded snout.

Gecko Eyes

Geckos that are active at night usually have eyes like a cat's, with thin vertical pupils. Geckos that are active during the day have more rounded pupils. Geckos have clear shields over their eyes. They clean the eye shields with their flat, fleshy tongues.

The body of a gecko is either rounded or flat. The gecko's skin is soft and feels a little like velvet. The skin is very thin and delicate. Some geckos have skin that tears like wet paper.

A gecko's scales do not overlap as they do on many other reptiles. Some geckos have pointed, spiky scales. But the scales are usually soft.

Powerful Limbs

A gecko's limbs are well developed and very powerful. They allow a gecko to jump and land without injury. Geckos can also move around quickly. That skill is useful when they are trying to avoid hungry **predators**.

Some geckos have thin eyes like a cat's.

16

A gecko's toes are the key to its ability to hang on to things. On the bottom of each toe are rows of thin plates called **lamellae**. Within each of these rows are dozens of tiny hook-shaped cells. The **microscopic** hooks catch onto anything. This allows the gecko to crawl on walls, ceilings, and even smooth surfaces like mirrors and window panes. Geckos also have claws that help them climb trees.

Gecko Tails

A gecko's tail is usually smaller than its body. It has many purposes. It is a tool of defense. If a hungry predator slaps its paw down on a gecko's tail, the tail will break off. This is called **autotomy**. Most lizards wait until the tail is grabbed. Geckos can drop their tails even before they are touched.

The tail bones have cracks in them. The gecko uses its muscles to break the bones. The gecko runs away and the tail stays behind. The tail continues to thrash for several minutes.

Geckos' tails grow back when they are broken off.

While the predator eats the tail, the gecko escapes. The gecko's tail will slowly grow back. But it will not be as perfect as the original tail.

Finally, the tail acts as a storage area. When a gecko eats, fat and water are stored at the base of the tail. They are ready for use if food or drink become hard to find.

Most geckos are brown, yellow, or gray. And most have a pattern. A few geckos are just one color. Others have beautiful combinations of red, green, and even blue. A few **diurnal** geckos can change color.

Geckos can store food in their tails

Chapter 4

Daily Life

Most geckos sleep during the day and are active at night. This means they are nocturnal. A few geckos sleep during the night and are active during the day. They are diurnal animals.

Most geckos are arboreal. That means they spend most of their time in trees and bushes. Some geckos are terrestrial. That means they spend most of their time on the ground.

Like most reptiles, geckos spend a lot of time **basking** in the sun. They do this because they are **cold-blooded**. They need the sun's heat to survive. Their bodies cannot make their

Most geckos live in trees.

own heat. Instead, they have to get their warmth from the sun.

Chase Insects

Geckos are quick and alert hunters. They chase and catch their food. Most geckos live on a diet of insects. They eat beetles, ants, flies, crickets, and spiders.

Some geckos also eat a little plant life. But that is usually because the insect they ate was sitting on a leaf. They ate the leaf along with the insect. Large geckos also eat small rodents, small birds, and even other lizards.

When they are thirsty, most geckos lick drops of rain or dew from leaves and branches. Although most reptiles drink only water, many geckos also like fruit juices. When rotten fruits fall from trees, geckos will climb down and lick them dry. It is a sweet and nutritious drink for the geckos.

Many Sounds

Most lizards can only hiss or make a simple sound. Geckos are different. They make many

Most geckos eat insects.

sounds. They can squeak, click, croak, and
even bark.

Geckos are bold and aggressive fighters.
They can inflict painful, bloody wounds. They
are considered food by snakes, other lizards,
large cats, and many birds. Gecko battles are
often ones of life or death.

Chapter 5

Reproduction

Geckos mate at different times of the year. It depends on where they live. Those that live in the north usually breed in the spring. But some mate in both the spring and the fall.

Those that live in the south may breed at any time of year. But most breed right after the **rainy season**. This often occurs during the fall and sometimes during the winter. Many tropical geckos mate more than once a year.

Geckos lay eggs. Sometimes the developing eggs can actually be seen bulging out the sides of the pregnant mothers. Usually only two eggs are laid per **clutch**. But many geckos lay more

Geckos get together during the mating season.

Delicate Skin

Food-Storing Tail

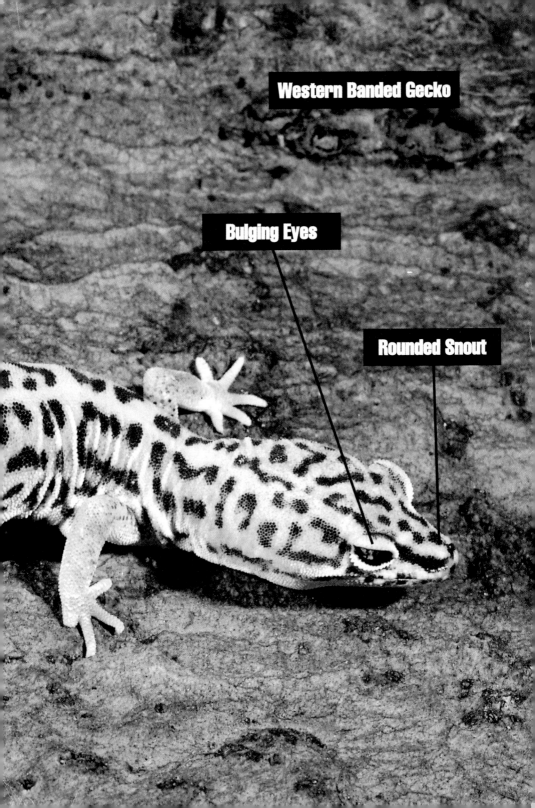

Western Banded Gecko

Bulging Eyes

Rounded Snout

Some animals like to eat young geckos such as this ashy gecko hatchling.

than one clutch per year. Some lay as many as three or four clutches per year.

Some animals like to eat gecko eggs. To keep her eggs safe from predators, a pregnant gecko tries to find a dark and quiet place to drop her clutch. Sometimes a group of mothers will use the same spot year after year.

Small Eggs

A gecko's eggs are about the size of a jellybean. The eggs are soft, white, and very sticky. A mother gecko can attach her eggs to just about any surface. She may stick the eggs to trees, leaves, or rocks. The eggs harden after they have been attached to something. Then the stickiness dries up.

Gecko eggs are hardy. They are hardier than most lizard eggs. Gecko eggs can stand a great amount of temperature change. It usually takes a gecko egg from two to six months to hatch.

Sometimes gecko eggs are stuck to packing crates. Then they are shipped all over the world. If the climate and food are right, the baby gecko that hatched in the new location will be fine.

The average life span of a gecko varies from species to species. But most geckos will live from four to 12 years. The oldest gecko on record lived 23 years.

Chapter 6

Conservation

Many of the world's animals are disappearing. Trees are being cut down for lumber and to make room for farms, buildings, and other development. People are taking up more and more space. Habitat destruction is causing many species to die out.

There are, however, many **conservation** groups trying to help geckos and other animals. Most gecko populations are still very stable. Geckos are able to survive because they adapt to the changes.

Geckos help people by eating many insects. When there are geckos around, the number of insects is very low.

Geckos survive by adapting to the environment.

Hundreds of thousands of geckos have been kept as pets or studied in laboratories all over the world. Some keepers have bred them in captivity. Geckos usually do very well in large terrariums. But they usually do not become tame enough to handle.

Zoo Trips

If you cannot view geckos in the wild or keep them as pets, visit a zoo. A zoo is a great place to learn about lizards and other animals.

Make the most of your zoo trips. Do not just walk around aimlessly. Leave knowing more than you did before your visit.

Take a notebook with you. When you see a lizard that interests you, stand quietly. Watch the lizard. See what it does. Then write down what you see. You can learn a lot about an animal by doing this.

Ask yourself questions. Is the lizard sleeping during the day? If so, it is probably nocturnal. Is the lizard in a cage by itself? Then it probably is a solitary animal and does not usually live in a group. How big is the lizard?

You can see a gecko's toes close-up at the zoo.

What color is it? How does it act? You will be amazed at how much you can learn by observation.

If you can, bring a camera with you. A zoo is an excellent place to take pictures of animals. Lizards are beautiful animals. If you are a good artist, sketch pictures during your zoo trip. Photos and drawings of lizards give you visual reminders of your trip. You could put the pictures in a scrapbook and use them later for school projects.

Some of the top zoos in which to view lizards are in Houston, Philadelphia, San Diego, and Washington, D.C. In Canada, two of the top zoos are in Calgary and Toronto. But there are many other wonderful zoos, too. Visit a zoo and enjoy yourself. Trips to the zoo are both fun and educational.

Look for the golddust day gecko at the zoo.

Some of the top zoos in which to view lizards

Black Hills Reptile Gardens
South Highway 16
Rapid City, SD 57701

Calgary Zoo
1300 Zoo Road NE
P.O. Box 3036 Station B
Calgary, AB T2M 4R8
Canada

Houston Zoological Gardens
1513 Outer Belt Drive
Houston, TX 77030

Metropolitan Toronto Zoo
361A Old Finch Avenue
Scarborough, ON M1B 5K7
Canada

National Zoological Park
3001 Connecticut Avenue NW
Washington, DC 20008

The Philadelphia Zoological Garden
34th Street and Girard Avenue
Philadelphia, PA 19020

The San Diego Zoo
Park Boulevard and Zoo Avenue
Balboa Park
San Diego, CA 92103

Look for the velvet gecko at the zoo.

Glossary

autotomy—the reflex action by which a lizard's tail is broken off at a special joint

bask—lie or rest and enjoy a pleasant warmth

carnivore—animal that eats the flesh of other animals

class—group of animals or plants that have similar characteristics, ranking above an order and below a phylum

clutch—a nest of eggs

cold-blooded—having a body temperature that changes according to the temperature of the surroundings

conservation—the official care, protection, or management of natural resources

diurnal—active during the day rather than at night

family—group of related plants or animals, ranking above a genus and below an order

genus—group of closely related plants or animals, usually including several species

habitat—area in which an animal normally lives

lamellae—thin plates that extend across the underside of the toes on many lizards

microscopic—too small to be seen by the eye alone but visible through a microscope

New World—the Western Hemisphere

nocturnal—active at night rather than during the day

Old World—the Eastern Hemisphere

order—group of plants or animals that are similar in many ways, ranking above a family and below a class

phylum—one of the larger groups into which plants and animals are divided, ranking above a class and below a kingdom

predator—animal that lives by capturing and feeding on other animals

rainy season—period of the year marked by rainstorms that usually are warm, heavy, and continuous

range—geographical area in which a particular animal is found

scientific classification system—the way all living things are listed and categorized

species—group of plants or animals most closely related in the scientific classification system

To Learn More

Barrett, Norman. *Dragons and Lizards.* New York: Franklin Watts, 1991.

Chace, G. Earl. *The World of Lizards.* New York: Dodd, Mead and Co., 1982.

Gravelle, Karen. *Lizards.* New York: Franklin Watts, 1991.

Ivy, Bill. *Lizards. Our Wildlife World.* Danbury, Conn.: Grolier, 1990.

McCarthy, Colin. *Reptile. An Eyewitness Book.* New York: Alfred A. Knopf, 1991.

Schnieper, Claudia. *Lizards.* Minneapolis: Carolrhoda Books, 1988.

Smith, Trevor. *Amazing Lizards.* New York: Alfred A. Knopf, 1991.

You can read about geckos in *Reptile Hobbyist* and *Reptile and Amphibian* magazines.

Many geckos like to live in people's houses.

Useful Addresses

Charles Darwin Foundation for the Galápagos Isles
National Zoological Park
Washington, DC 20008

The Long Island Herpetological Society
476 North Ontario Avenue
Lindenhurst, NY 11757

Minnesota Herpetological Society
Bell Museum of Natural History
10 Church Street SE
Minneapolis, MN 55455-0104

Ontario Herpetological Society
P.O. Box 244
Port Credit, ON L5G 4L8
Canada

National Wildlife Federation
1400 Sixteenth Street NW
Washington, DC 20036

The Nature Conservancy
1815 North Lynn Street
Arlington, VA 22209

Rainforest Alliance
270 Lafayette Street
Suite 512
New York, NY 10012

San Diego Herpetological Society
P.O. Box 4036
San Diego, CA 92164-4036

World Nature Association
P.O. Box 673
Silver Spring, MD 20918

Internet Sites

Gekko Gecko Site
http://huizen.dds.nl/~phelsuma

Heatherk's Gecko Page
http://www.wttf.com/~gecko

Herp Link
http://home.ptd.net/~herplink/index.html

ZooNet
http://www.mindspring.com/~zoonet

The wall gecko blends in with its environment.

Index

Africa, 11
Amazon, 9
Antarctica, 5, 11
ants, 5, 24
Asia, 11
Australia, 11

beetles, 5, 24

Canada, 36, 38, 44
class, 8, 40, 41
cold-blooded, 23, 40
crickets, 5, 24

deserts, 5, 9, 12
diurnal, 21, 23, 40

Europe, 11

family, 4, 9, 40, 41
flies, 5, 24

genus, 9, 40

lamellae, 4, 18, 40

Malaysian, 7

New World, 11, 41
New Zealand, 15
nocturnal, 23, 35, 41
North America, 11

Old World, 11, 41
order, 9, 40, 41

phylum, 8, 40, 41

rain forests, 5, 12

Saint George Island, 9
scientific classification
   system, 7, 41
snakes, 9, 25
South America, 11
species, 9, 11, 31, 33, 40, 41
spiders, 5, 24

zoo, 35, 36, 38, 39, 44, 46